The Cold War

Sean Sheehan

First published by Hodder Wayland
338 Euston Road, London NW1 3BH, United Kingdom
Hodder Wayland is an imprint of Hodder Children's Books, a division of Hodder Headline Limited.
This edition published under license from Hodder Children's Books. All rights reserved.

Produced for Hodder Wayland by White-Thomson Publishing Ltd.
2/3 St. Andrew's Place, Lewes BN7 1UP, United Kingdom
Copyright © 2003 White-Thomson Publishing Ltd.

Editor: Anna Lee, Designer: Jamie Asher, Consultant: Scott Lucas, Proofreader: Philippa Smith,
Photo researcher: Shelley Noronha (Glass Onion Pictures)

Published in the United States by Smart Apple Media
1980 Lookout Drive, North Mankato, Minnesota 56003

Library of Congress Cataloging-in-Publication Data

Sheehan, Sean, 1951– The Cold War / Sean Sheehan.
p. cm. — (Questioning history)
Summary: Discusses the principal causes and events of the Cold War, the period from 1945 to 1991
when the United States and the Soviet Union kept each other in check through mutual fear and distrust, and considers what the outcome might have been had different decisions been made at crucial
points during this time.
ISBN 1-58340-266-7
1. Cold War—Juvenile literature. 2. World politics—1945–1989—Juvenile literature. 3. United States—
Foreign relations—Soviet Union—Juvenile literature. 4. Soviet Union—Foreign relations—United
States—Juvenile literature. [1. Cold War. 2. World politics—1945–1989. 3. United States—Foreign
relations—Soviet Union. 4. Soviet Union—Foreign relations—United States.] I. Title. II. Series.

D843 .S4523 2003   909.82'5—dc21   2002036589

9 8 7 6 5 4 3 2 1

Picture credits: AKG, 32; Camera Press, 14, 21, 22, 30, 41, 43, 45, 46, 52; Corbis, 4, 10; Impact, 53;
Mary Evans, 9; Novosti, title page, 47, 49, 54; Peter Newark's Military Pictures, 5, 7, 8, 18, 19, 29, 33,
40; Popperphoto, 25, 26, 35, 39, 51, 56, 57, 58; Topham, 16, 36, 37, 48, 50; maps on 11, 13, and 15 by
Nick Hawken; maps on 20, 24, and 28 by The Map Studio

CONTENTS

CHAPTER 1

Who Started the Cold War?

The Cold War is the name given to the period from 1945 to 1991 when a high level of distrust existed between two superpowers: the United States and the Soviet Union (also called the USSR). The Cold War dominated world events because each of the two superpowers tried to influence the world in ways that suited its own interests. These interests were based on very different ideas about the organization of society, which led to each side fearing the other.

BELOW *Leaders of the USSR, U.S., and Britain meet for the last time at the Potsdam Conference in July 1945. Their agreement to divide a defeated Germany into different zones of occupation would, unknowingly, set the stage for the outbreak of the Cold War.*

GLOBAL CONFLICT

The Cold War also led to a series of conflicts in different parts of the world where the two superpowers found themselves in confrontation. In some of these situations, the state of mutual fear led to a dangerous level of tension because each superpower possessed many nuclear weapons. However, despite some close calls, the conflict never developed into a

state of direct armed war between the U.S. and the USSR. Such a direct war would have been a "hot" war, and, because this never happened, the standoff between the U.S. and the USSR continued to be called the Cold War.

The Cold War lasted for some 45 years, and over the course of this time it involved conflicts in more parts of the world than World War II. In Central and South America, in Africa and the Middle East, and in central and southeast Asia, real wars caused by the Cold War led to the deaths of millions of people. The course of world events was shaped by the Cold War, and even after it had ended, the consequences continued to influence events in different parts of the world.

ABOVE *Each side in the Cold War regarded its own economic and social system as superior to the other. This cartoon is an example of how the USSR saw the economic systems of the U.S. and Britain, with ordinary working people as the victims of capitalism.*

? **WHAT IF...**

There was a World War III?

There were moments during the Cold War when there was a very real risk that one of the superpowers would launch an attack on the other side using nuclear weapons. It is very likely that this would have brought a counterattack, unleashing more nuclear weapons. The countries of Europe, as allies of one of the superpowers or the other, would have been involved, and possibly other regions of the world. The result could have been World War III. What if this had happened? Given that the U.S. and the USSR had enough weapons to destroy the world and all life on it several times over, World War III would have threatened the survival of civilization as we know it.

THE COLD WAR STARTS

On April 25, 1945, American soldiers crossed the Elbe River in Germany to meet with Russian soldiers from the Union of Soviet Socialist Republics (USSR). They hugged each other in joy and danced together to celebrate their joint victory over Nazi Germany. The armies of both countries had fought their separate ways across Germany. The Americans came from the west after landing in northern France on D-Day, and the Soviet army came from the east after beating back Hitler's invasion of their country. Now they had come together in a symbolic moment that represented the defeat of Nazism and the end of World War II.

? EVENT IN QUESTION

The Cold War: Whose history?

As with any historical event, there are various aspects to the Cold War over which historians do not agree. However, in the case of recent conflicts such as the Cold War, the different opinions held by historians may be affected by the fact that they grew up during the period in question. The following points are worth considering when reading about the Cold War.

• Who is writing? It is worth looking at any information provided about the author's background and experience. Even professional historians interpret aspects of the Cold War in different ways, and an account by an American, for example, could be quite different from one by a Russian.
• When was it written? Was it written during the Cold War, when perhaps it was more difficult to step back and view what happened as a part of history? If it was written after the mid-1990s, the author may have had access to information that wasn't previously available.

The political leaders of the Allies (nations opposing Germany) had met during the war to discuss their common goal of defeating Germany. On July 17, 1945, they came together for their last war conference amid the ruins of Berlin, Germany's capital city, but there was no hugging or dancing. Despite having supported each other during the war against a common enemy, there had been an earlier history of mistrust, and this now began to make itself felt once again. The deep mistrust went back to the consequences of a revolution in Russia in 1917 that led to a communist government and, later, the creation of the USSR. This communist government abolished private property and claimed it would build a new society based on ideas of social and economic equality for all.

ABOVE *Comrades-in-arms. Soviet and American soldiers first met on April 25 at Torgau on the Elbe River in Germany. Two days later, when this photograph was taken, they repeated their joyful meeting for the cameras.*

COMMUNISM AND THE WEST

The idea of communism frightened countries such as Britain and the U.S., whose rulers thought the 1917 Russian revolution might lead to similar revolutions in their own countries. After the 1917 revolution, they had invaded Russia and tried unsuccessfully to depose the new government. It was 1933 before the U.S. established diplomatic relations with the Soviet Union, and the alliance between the two countries during World War II was more a matter of convenience than anything else. The U.S. transported tanks and other aid to Russia to help defeat Germany. Yet despite this, the USSR remained suspicious of the U.S. and Britain, feeling they should have made their D-Day landing in

RIGHT *This poster from World War II, showing the Union Jack, the Stars and Stripes, and the Hammer and Sickle in the foreground, celebrates the fact that Britain, the U.S., the USSR, and other nations were allies fighting on the same side.*

Western Europe at least a year earlier. The Soviet Union felt, with some justification, that it had been left to withstand the Nazi war machine alone.

ABOVE *Soviet troops drive past the Austrian parliament building in Vienna on their way to western Germany in April 1945.*

THE SUPERPOWERS

The national wealth of the U.S. was greater after the war than at any stage before. The country produced more than half of the world's total manufactured goods and owned two-thirds of the world's gold. The USSR also emerged in the post-war world as a superpower. Despite having lost some 27 million citizens in defeating Germany, the Soviet Union had a powerful, undefeated, and huge army. It was now determined to make sure that never again would its land be invaded from the west. As its army moved across Europe toward Berlin, attempts were made to set up governments that would be friendly toward the USSR (see map on page 15).

? PEOPLE IN QUESTION

Joseph Stalin (1879–1953)

Joseph Stalin became ruler of the USSR in 1924, and in 1945 he was determined to keep the Soviet Union safe from the threat of any future invasion. He made it clear that neighboring countries such as Poland would not be allowed to have governments unless they were firm allies of the Soviet Union. The U.S. was not trusted, and the Marshall Plan (see page 12) was seen as an excuse for America to extend its economic power.

The West did not understand Stalin's preoccupation with the future security of his country. According to some historians, the aggressive attitude of the USSR about building a firm defense against the West contributed to the beginning of the Cold War.

POST-WAR EUROPE

Britain emerged from the war as a virtually bankrupt country, dependent on financial support from the U.S., which now wielded the global power once held by Britain. The defeated nations of Japan and Germany were in a state of economic and political collapse. In 1945, Germany was divided between the Allies in what was planned as a temporary measure until a non-Nazi government could be formed. The city of Berlin, which lay in the eastern half of the country, was also divided between the Allies. Meanwhile, France and Italy, both very weak and in need of economic assistance, had popular communist parties that looked to the USSR as their model. There was no dominant power in Europe, and if communist parties were elected to government in France and Italy, they would be friendly toward the USSR.

BELOW *Cities such as Berlin, shown here in 1946, had to be literally rebuilt after World War II.*

This situation alarmed the U.S. because America wanted to promote its idea of freedom, which meant an economic system built on private enterprise and the rights of people to travel freely. Soviet society was based on the idea that the common good was more important than freedom of the individual, and the country's wealth was owned by the government. These differences resulted in the USSR becoming preoccupied by a need to protect itself against any future threat to its security from Western Europe. The situation in defeated Germany after 1945 meant that the U.S. and the USSR were on a collision course, driven by their different priorities.

ABOVE *After World War II, Germany was divided into areas occupied by the USSR, Britain, the U.S., and France. The inset map shows the three air corridors between Berlin and the West.*

? PEOPLE IN QUESTION

*Harry S. Truman
(1884–1972)*

Harry Truman became President of the United States in April 1945, and it was soon made clear that his administration would adopt a hard-line attitude toward the USSR. Truman was convinced by the arguments of many of his advisers, who said that the Soviet Union could not be trusted and that it would try to expand its power and threaten the American way of life. Truman declared there was a clash of values between "alternative ways of life" and that the Soviet Union needed to be contained. This aggressive attitude, which became known as the Truman Doctrine, has been seen by some historians as contributing to the development of the Cold War.

WHO WAS RESPONSIBLE FOR THE COLD WAR?

Historians do not agree over who started the Cold War, but many see both the U.S. and the USSR as being responsible in different ways. The beginning of the Cold War was like a game of ping pong, with each side responding to a move made by its opponent. One of the first moves occurred when the U.S. decided to strengthen the economies of countries in Western Europe and win their support with the Marshall Plan. Named after the then U.S. Secretary of State, George Marshall, and announced in 1947, this plan devoted huge amounts of money to dealing with the food shortage and lack of industrial production in Europe. Six months later, a new American government organization called the Central Intelligence Agency (CIA) secretly channelled millions of dollars to opposition parties in Italy to prevent a communist party from winning a general election that took place there in 1948.

The USSR became even more suspicious of the U.S. when details of the Marshall Plan emerged. The Soviets pressured eastern European countries to create communist governments, and in the case of Czechoslovakia the communist party created enough disorder to scare its president into allowing a communist government to be formed. The U.S. responded by discussing with Britain the idea of a military alliance in Western Europe, which eventually led to the North

? WHAT IF...

The superpowers had been less suspicious?

If the two superpowers had been less suspicious of each other, perhaps the Cold War could have been avoided. Stalin could have accepted the Marshall Plan instead of viewing it as an American ploy to dominate Europe and threaten the USSR. The Truman administration could have tried to understand the Soviet Union's need to defend itself against another invasion, instead of acting as if the USSR was intent on taking over the world and threatening America. Perhaps the leaders of the two superpowers were too alike and too willing to see the world from only their points of view. Were the superpowers too quick to act in ways that were seen by the other side as threatening, and too stubborn to make concessions and reach an agreement? Or were they acting in the best interests of their country?

Atlantic Treaty Organization (NATO) in 1949. Six years later, the Soviet Union formed the Warsaw Pact, a similar military grouping based around the USSR and the eastern European states with communist governments.

THE DIVISION OF GERMANY

Events in Germany made it clear that Europe was being divided into a pro-American part and a pro-USSR part. The hostility that was developing between the U.S. and the USSR led to Germany being divided into two different states: East Germany and West Germany. By 1949, the USSR had its own nuclear weapons. The stage was set for an international conflict, and the Cold War was underway.

? EVENT IN QUESTION

Dividing Germany: Who was responsible?

In 1948, a new common currency was introduced in the western half of Germany with the support of the U.S. The Soviets responded by introducing a currency of their own. The USSR, applying pressure in order to prevent the western currency from being used in Berlin, kept food and supplies from western Germany from reaching western Berlin. The U.S. responded by flying in the necessary supplies until the blockade was lifted. From one point of view, the USSR showed its aggressive intentions by blockading western Berlin. From another point of view, the USSR was provoked by the threat of a new currency that would bring all of Berlin under Western, non-Soviet influence. Either way, Germany was divided into a communist East Germany and a capitalist West Germany.

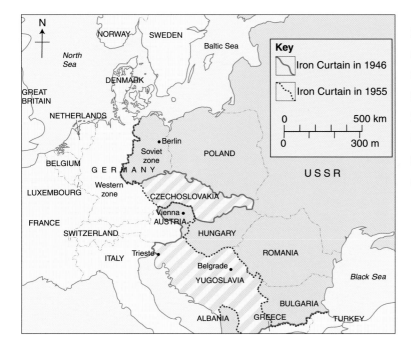

Key

Iron Curtain in 1946

Iron Curtain in 1955

0 — 500 km

0 — 300 m

LEFT *The British prime minister, Winston Churchill, described the border between Soviet-dominated Eastern Europe and the democracies of the West as an "Iron Curtain."*

CHAPTER 2

Theaters of War

The scene of action in a war is sometimes described as a theater of war, and because the Cold War was played out in a variety of places and situations, many different theaters of war developed. Often only one of the two superpowers was involved in a theater of war, using force to protect what it regarded as its area of influence. This was the case in Eastern Europe and in parts of South and Central America and Africa. In some places—Cuba being the most dramatic example—both the U.S. and the USSR found themselves directly involved. In this kind of situation there was always the possibility that the theater of war would broaden into a direct and very dangerous conflict between the two superpowers.

BELOW *Soviet troops and tanks enter Budapest, the capital of Hungary, in November 1956. In the street fighting that followed, around 3,500 Hungarians were killed and 200,000 fled the country.*

Both Cold War superpowers used their military might to control neighboring states. In 1956, when Hungary tried to establish an independent, non-communist government, Nikita Kruschev, leader of the Soviet Union, sent in tanks, and thousands of Hungarians were killed. When in 1968 some communist leaders, in what was then Czechoslovakia, tried to introduce liberal reforms, Soviet tanks once again rolled into the country and took control. The U.S. did not intervene in either of these situations, accepting the fact that these countries came under the Soviet sphere of control. In a similar way, the USSR did not intervene when the U.S., feeling that Central America was in its own sphere of influence, acted there to protect its interests. In 1965, the Dominican Republic was successfully invaded to restore a government friendly toward America. In 1983, the Caribbean island of Grenada was also invaded because its new government was regarded as unfriendly to the U.S.

BELOW *A force of nearly 2,000 U.S. troops invade Grenada in 1983, resulting in some 400 Grenadian casualties and a new pro-American government.*

? EVENT IN QUESTION

The Berlin Wall: A safeguard against war?

Although the Wall changed the lives of many East Germans, Berliners had little choice but to accept its existence. Much of the rest of the world regarded the Wall as a physical symbol of the tyrannical nature of communism. However, it was also seen as a way of avoiding a direct military confrontation between the two superpowers. While the Wall separated families and friends and limited personal freedom, it also kept the armed forces of the U.S. and the USSR apart. Some people felt that the chances of an open war were therefore reduced.

THE BERLIN WALL

While the Marshall Plan helped West Germany's economy to prosper, East Germany suffered from a lack of investment, and the economy never flourished. This made many East Germans want to leave for West Germany. It was not an easy task because barbed wire fences with armed guards, erected by East Germany, marked the boundary between the two parts of Germany. Within Berlin, however, people could move between the different sectors with little difficulty. The easiest way for East Germans to leave their country was by slipping into East Berlin and then crossing over to the western part of the city.

As refugees, East Germans could either stay in West Berlin or ask to be flown out to other West German cities. By 1961, nearly three million citizens had left East Germany. If this was allowed to continue, there was a danger of the East German economy collapsing altogether. The Soviet leader, Nikita Krushchev, met the new American president, John F. Kennedy, in June 1961, but they were unable to reach any agreement over Berlin. Within a couple of months, the East German government

RIGHT *Conrad Schumann, a 19-year-old soldier reporting for duty as an East German border guard on August 15, 1961, took his chance to escape to the West when the other guards had their backs turned. He joined his family, who had fled earlier.*

began building a barrier of barbed wire between the two halves of Berlin. This soon became a wall, with armed guards under orders to shoot anyone who tried to leave East Berlin without permission. Berlin was to remain a divided city for the next 28 years.

? PEOPLE IN QUESTION

Nikita Khruschev
(1894–1971)

There are differences of opinion about the role of Nikita Khruschev, a leader of the USSR (1953–64), in the Cold War. While he made some steps toward giving his people more freedom, such as releasing political prisoners, he was also determined to maintain control over Eastern Europe. Like U.S. President John F. Kennedy, Khruschev had some advisers who wanted the USSR to adopt an aggressive attitude toward the U.S. and meet any threats of force with a show of equal force. And like Kennedy, Khruschev sought out a peaceful compromise to the crisis that developed over Cuba (see pages 18–19). Khruschev's resolve to avoid war was seen, however, as a mark of weakness. Two years later, he fell from power after losing the support of political and military leaders in his own country.

A DIVIDED EUROPE

In time, the division of Europe as a whole came to be regarded as an unavoidable consequence of the Cold War. The international borders that divided Western Europe from Eastern Europe were accepted as representing the division of the continent into areas of American and Soviet influence. Each side protected its territory with powerful armies numbering millions of soldiers, and each side possessed fearsome nuclear weapons. A very dangerous kind of stability emerged, mainly because it came to be accepted that any military showdown in Europe would very probably mean the destruction of the continent in a nuclear war. This never came to pass, but many other parts of the world did become theaters of war. In the case of Cuba, the world came close to a direct, armed conflict between the superpowers.

THE CUBAN MISSILE CRISIS

The USSR claimed that land on its side of the "Iron Curtain" should remain under Soviet influence. In a similar kind of way, the U.S. regarded the islands in the Caribbean Sea as land that should remain under its influence. This attitude on the part of the U.S. went back long before the Cold War. So when in 1959 a corrupt dictatorship ruling Cuba was overthrown in a popular revolution, the U.S. was concerned about the island's future. This was especially true when Cuba's new socialist government, under its leader Fidel Castro, nationalized parts of the economy in which American companies had invested.

In March 1961, the CIA organized an invasion of Cuba by 1,500 Cuban exiles to depose Castro, but it was a complete failure. The U.S. then cut off trade with Cuba, so Castro looked to the USSR as a trading partner. What happened next was a major incident in the Cold War, and one that very nearly brought about World War III.

The U.S. had nuclear weapons in Italy and Britain and some fairly obsolete ones in Turkey, a country that shared a border with the USSR. In 1961, Castro agreed to Khruschev's plan to secretly place Soviet nuclear missiles in Cuba. U.S. leaders grew alarmed when they discovered that Soviet ships were bringing missiles to Cuba. Any missiles launched from Cuba

BELOW *Fidel Castro (seated), photographed in 1957 in the Sierra Maestra mountains in Cuba during a campaign that ended with the removal of Fulgencio Batista, a corrupt dictator who had ruled the island for 25 years.*

would be close enough to the U.S. to score a direct hit. America responded by declaring a state of nuclear readiness, preparing its armory for nuclear war, and mounting a blockade of the sea so that no more Soviet ships carrying missiles could reach Cuba. The ships had orders to continue on their course, and a confrontation leading to war seemed about to happen.

The world held its breath as the superpower leaders discussed what to do. After many days of uncertainty, a deal was struck. The missiles were withdrawn by the Soviet Union in return for a guarantee from the U.S. not to invade Cuba. Also, although this was kept secret from the public, the U.S. agreed to later withdraw its own missiles from Turkey. Both the American and Soviet public saw the removal of the missiles from Cuba as a humiliating defeat for the USSR.

BELOW *Kennedy and Khruschev shake hands at a summit meeting in Vienna in June 1961. Within 18 months, they were on the verge of unleashing World War III.*

? WHAT IF...

Kennedy and Khruschev had not made a deal?

At some point, nuclear weapons would probably have been used. Which side might have first fired a nuclear weapon seems irrelevant given the mutual destruction it would have unleashed. The avoidance of war was a very close call. U.S. Defense Secretary Robert McNamara later recalled leaving a crisis meeting "on a beautiful fall evening . . . into the open air to look and to smell it, because I thought it was the last Saturday I would ever see." That same evening, one of Khrushev's advisers, convinced that Moscow would be hit by nuclear bombs, called his wife to warn her to leave the city immediately.

CENTRAL AND SOUTH AMERICA

The Cuban crisis was unusual because it led to a direct confrontation between the U.S. and the USSR and raised the stakes of the Cold War by making a nuclear war the likely outcome of such a confrontation. For the most part, however, the Cold War was played out across the world in a less spectacular manner. Central and South America became one such theater of war that lasted from the 1950s to the 1990s.

GUATEMALA

Central and South America became involved in the Cold War in 1954 when the CIA successfully deposed the elected government of Guatemala. Large areas of uncultivated land belonging mostly to an American company had been nationalized in Guatemala and distributed to landless peasants. The CIA trained and financed a force of Guatemalans who overthrew the government and installed a military dictator in power. The nationalized land was taken back, and hundreds of left-wing (communist) supporters were executed.

RIGHT *Many of the independent states of Central America, partly because of their proximity to the U.S., became battlegrounds during the Cold War.*

CHILE

Something similar took place in Chile, where a socialist government under President Salvador Allende was elected in 1970. Land was nationalized and distributed to poor farmers, and industries were also nationalized. The U.S. worked secretly to destabilize the country, prevent economic assistance from reaching the government, and encourage a military overthrow of Allende. In 1973, there was a military takeover by General Augusto Pinochet, Allende was killed, and hundreds of thousands of left-wing supporters were rounded up. Many supporters were executed, and many more were never seen again, becoming known as "the disappeared." As in Guatemala, the nationalized land was taken away from farmers under Pinochet's military rule, and nationalized industries were returned to their private owners.

Augusto Pinochet (1915–)

After overthrowing President Allende, Augusto Pinochet closed the Chilean parliament and established a military regime. More than 3,000 Allende supporters are believed to have been killed by Pinochet's forces, and thousands more tortured. However, Pinochet always maintained that he acted as a patriot and rescued his country from the threat of communism. As Chile's economy improved, many Chileans came to support this view. In October 1998, Pinochet was arrested on charges relating to human rights abuses during his years in power. The case was suspended in July 2001 due to his poor health.

BELOW *General Pinochet, who ruled Chile between 1973 and 1990 after deposing the elected government, boasted in 1975, "Never a leaf moves in Chile without my knowing of it."*

NICARAGUA

In Nicaragua, the largest country in Central America, the U.S. had an ally in the Somoza government. The Somoza family ruled over an extremely poor country and became very rich through corruption. By 1979, after a bitter civil war, Somoza was overthrown, and a left-wing government was formed by rebels called the Sandinistas. They began improving life for Nicaraguans and received support from Cuba. By 1981, another civil war had broken out, and the Contras, a group trying to depose the Sandinistas, turned to the U.S. for support. The CIA armed and trained the Contras and in 1984

BELOW *The fighters that opposed Nicaragua's left-wing government were* contrarevolutionarios *known as the Contras. With U.S. aid, they grew from a force of a few hundred to about 15,000 between 1982 and 1985.*

organized a plot to mine the ports of Nicaragua. This resulted in damage to ships of other countries, and the U.S. Congress publicly withdrew support from the Contras. By secretly selling arms to Iran and using the money to aid the Contras, however, the White House maintained its policy of opposing the Sandinistas. This illegal operation, when it became known to the public in 1986, became known as the Iran-Contra scandal and caused severe embarrassment to the U.S. government.

EL SALVADOR

El Salvador, also in Central America, had a history similar to that of Nicaragua. A harsh military government was supported by the U.S., while a rebel army waged a guerrilla war. Many thousands of people were killed or became part of "the disappeared" as a result of government "death squads," and a civil war lasted for years with neither side able to achieve a decisive victory. In 1981, the military government received $36 million in aid from the U.S., and three years later this had risen to $197 million.

The civil war lasted 12 years and did not come to an end until 1992, after an estimated 75,000 people had been killed and $6 billion had been spent by the U.S. El Salvador is now a democratic republic, and the rebel army of the civil war period is a political party.

? EVENT IN QUESTION

U.S. intervention in Central and South America: Was the Cold War an excuse?

From one point of view, the Cold War was used by the U.S. as an excuse in Central and South America to depose any government that was not friendly to American business interests. Many countries in that part of the world suffered from poverty and from enormous differences between the rich and poor, and American-owned companies were seen to benefit from such inequalities. When left-wing governments tried to improve the lives of their citizens, the U.S. used the Cold War as an excuse to remove them from power, even if they were democratically elected. From another point of view, however, the U.S. was protecting its interests in an unstable part of the world where communism was a threat. Left-wing governments, it was argued, would not support the U.S. and would instead turn to the USSR for support. This, it was felt, would tip the world balance of power in favor of the USSR and ought to be resisted. Therefore, it was necessary to support governments friendly to the U.S., even if they were brutal dictatorships.

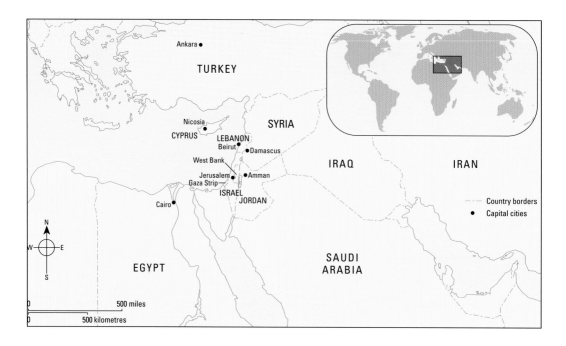

Ankara •

TURKEY

Nicosia
CYPRUS
LEBANON
Beirut • • Damascus
SYRIA
West Bank
Jerusalem • • Amman
Gaza Strip
ISRAEL
JORDAN
Cairo •

IRAQ

IRAN

N
W ⊕ E
S

------ Country borders
• Capital cities

EGYPT

SAUDI
ARABIA

500 miles
500 kilometres

ABOVE *Most of the*
Middle East was affected
by the course of the
Cold War. The West
Bank and the Gaza Strip
are Palestinian territories
but under the military
control of Israel.

THE MIDDLE EAST

The Cold War in Central and South America was affected by the region's closeness to the North American mainland, and by U.S. economic interests in that part of the world. In another theater of war, the Middle East, both the U.S. and the USSR shared similar concerns because of the region's rich supply of oil. In Iran in 1953, the CIA helped a U.S.-friendly party to depose the government and take power. The U.S. provided military and economic assistance, and in return, American oil companies and military advisers had a large presence in the country. This arrangement lasted until 1979, when a non-communist but anti-American Islamic government, under Ayatollah Khomeini, gained power in Iran.

ISRAEL

The U.S. also sought to make an ally of the state of Israel, a country that had come into existence in 1948. This angered Arab states—especially the Palestinians, whose land had been used to create the state of Israel. The stateless Palestinians lost more land in an Arab-Israeli war in 1967 and began to blame the U.S., who went on to support Israel with massive military and

? EVENT IN QUESTION

War in the Middle East: A consequence of the Cold War?

From one point of view, the Middle East was an unstable part of the world where the USSR sought to exercise its influence and have a say over a region that provided a major source of oil throughout the world. The U.S. supported Israel and built up its military strength so that the country could function as a deterrent to any Soviet plans for expansion in the Middle East. Therefore, war in the Middle East was a consequence of the Cold War. From another point of view, the Cold War was only part of the background, and the underlying conflict arose from the determination of both the U.S. and the USSR to try to maintain control over a valuable source of oil. Support for this point of view comes from the fact that the end of the Cold War did not bring war in the Middle East to an end. It is also true, however, that the situation in the Middle East is very complex and goes beyond the more straightforward conflict that fueled the Cold War.

economic aid. The USSR, meanwhile, sought to make allies of states such as Syria and Egypt through offers of aid, and in this way, the Middle East became another stage for the conflict of the Cold War. Another war between Israel, Syria, and Egypt in 1973 saw the opposing sides being armed and supported by the rival superpowers.

LEFT *Two U.S.-made Israeli tanks patrol East Jerusalem on June 10, 1967, six days after Israel launched an attack that led to the occupation of the Gaza Strip, the Golan Heights of Syria, and the West Bank and Arab sector of East Jerusalem.*

25

WAR IN AFRICA

Africa also became a focus for the deadly drama of the Cold War, and as with the Middle East, it had the effect of turning parts of the region into another theater of war. During the 1950s and 1960s, more than 30 new countries emerged in Africa as former colonial powers such as Britain bowed out in the face of demands for independence. The superpowers, each fearing that the other side would gain influence and power in the region, stepped in and chose different countries as allies. In the case of Angola in 1975, communist China as well as the U.S. and the USSR became involved in a conflict that cost

LEFT *A photo from the early days of Angola's civil war (1975–2002).*

many thousands of lives. The three powers gave military aid to different sides in a civil war that broke out in the country. Cuba and South Africa also became involved by sending in troops that fought with one another.

THE ANC AND SOUTH AFRICA

The USSR was able to appeal to nationalist groups in different parts of Africa on the grounds that communism supported their demands for independence and equality. This resulted in the African National Congress (ANC), a guerrilla force opposed to the white minority ruling South Africa, regarding the USSR as more of an ally than the U.S. Another result was that the U.S. remained on close terms with a racist state that denied equal rights to the black majority population (see panel) in a system called apartheid.

? WHAT IF...

The Cold War had never reached South Africa?

It is possible that, without the Cold War, apartheid would have ended in South Africa sooner than it finally did in the early 1990s. While the Cold War lasted, the U.S. felt there was a good reason to support South Africa, because it defended capitalism and allied itself with the West. Toward the end of the 1980s, when the Cold War was drawing to a close, the attitude of the U.S., as well as other Western countries and international banks, started to change. They began to put pressure on the white South African government to dismantle the system of apartheid and reach an agreement with the ANC.

The drawing to a close of the Cold War also changed the ANC. Some groups within the African National Congress loosened their attachment to the USSR, and the economic policies of the ANC became less socialist. This did a great deal to convince the white government in South Africa that a peace agreement could be reached with the ANC.

CHAPTER 3

The Cold War in Asia

The Cold War had its origins in Europe after World War II, but, as has been seen, the conflict between the superpowers was also acted out in other parts of the world. Apart from nearly 200 people who were killed trying to cross the Berlin Wall, very few people died as a result of the Cold War in Europe. On the other hand, in addition to the hundreds of thousands killed in Central and South America and Africa, the number of victims who died on Cold War battlefields in Asia is counted in millions. It was in Asia that the Cold War created the conditions for open and prolonged warfare, causing death and destruction on a massive scale.

BELOW *During the Cold War, Russia, Kazakhstan, Uzbekistan, Kyrgyzstan, Turkmenistan, and Tajikistan were all part of the USSR.*

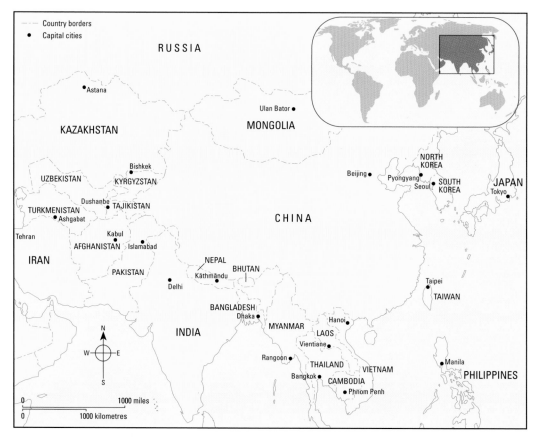

ABOVE *U.S. troops waiting for action atop an M26 tank in Korea in 1950.*

CHANGES IN ASIA

An important reason that the Cold War made itself felt so intensely in Asia is the history of that part of the world. Before World War II, much of the region had been colonized by European powers, but by 1945 the situation had changed radically. By successfully invading southeast Asia, the Japanese had exposed the weaknesses of European military control over its colonies. So, although Japan was eventually defeated, many Asian nations sought independence after World War II.

Former colonial rulers, mainly Britain and France, were no longer able to govern their empires as they once had. The region became unstable because the nature of the new governments that would replace the colonial powers remained uncertain.

? EVENT IN QUESTION

The end of colonialism in Asia

In its own way, the course of World War II set the stage for the Cold War in Asia just as it had done in Europe. Although finally defeated in 1945, Japan had launched a devastating attack on British Malaya in 1941 and captured the British-controlled island of Singapore early the following year. British prestige was dealt a severe blow because the Japanese had shown that Asians could defeat a Western imperial power. When the war was over, countries such as Vietnam and India, realizing that they need not remain the colonies of Western countries, began to demand independence. The cost of the war had weakened Britain and France financially, and they found it difficult after 1945 to bear the additional costs of resisting independence movements. This was the background to the instability in Asia, and it provided more theaters of war for the Cold War.

COMMUNISM IN ASIA

The largest of the unstable states in southeast Asia was China, a country that Japan had invaded and tried to control in the 1930s. In 1949, China became an independent communist state, and its leader, Mao Zedong, quickly established warm relations with the USSR. The prospect of an alliance between these two powerful states alarmed the West considerably, although, as it turned out, the USSR and China would later have a falling out. Equally alarming for the West was the fact that leaders of other national independence movements in Asia, seeking to replace the injustice of colonial rule, found a model for their hopes in the ideas of communism. In this way, their nationalist struggles for independence became entangled in the Cold War conflict.

BELOW *Celebrations in Tiananmen Square in Beijing on October 1, 1952, marking the third anniversary of Mao Zedong's announcement in the same square that "the Chinese people have now stood up."*

WAR IN KOREA

The first Asian country to suffer as a result of the Cold War was Korea. The country had been a Japanese colony during World War II before being liberated by Soviet and U.S. forces in 1945. They divided the country; a communist government ruled the north, while a non-communist government was established in the south. North Korea became an ally of the USSR, and its leader, Kim Il Sung, sought permission from Stalin to invade the South and unify the country as a communist state. This took place on June 25, 1950, and the U.S. reacted by calling on the United Nations (UN) to condemn the invasion.

At the time, the USSR was boycotting the UN because communist China was not being admitted as a member, and on June 27, the UN voted to defend South Korea by military force. The U.S., along with Britain and other allies, sent troops to fight the North Korean army, and a period of bitter warfare followed. In October, the scale of the war increased dramatically when China sent its own forces into the conflict. General Douglas MacArthur, who was commanding U.S. troops in Korea, was dismissed from his post after calling for the invasion and bombing of China.

? PEOPLE IN QUESTION

Douglas MacArthur (1880–1964)

General Douglas MacArthur, a celebrated hero of World War II, was placed in charge of military forces in Korea. He had always argued that the Cold War would be fought in Asia rather than Europe, and he welcomed the opportunity to lead a determined war against the enemy. Applying the logic of the Cold War, he called for the bombing of China as a way of achieving success in Korea. However, political leaders on both sides of the Cold War were learning to avoid an open war that might be difficult for either side to win. A general like MacArthur, who saw the Cold War in very military terms, was not acceptable, and he was dismissed. To some, MacArthur was a Cold War hero who spoke his mind; to others, he was a dangerous Cold War warrior who risked nuclear war.

? EVENT IN QUESTION

Did the Korean War achieve anything?

From one perspective, the invasion of South Korea was viewed as a clear instance of Soviet expansion that needed to be contained. If the invasion was not resisted militarily, it was reasoned, the Soviet Union would feel free to organize similar takeovers in other parts of Asia. From another perspective, however, it was only North Korea that wanted to invade in order to unify the country, and the USSR agreed to their ally's wishes because it didn't think the U.S. would go to war over it. The USSR had no plans to expand its influence and dominate the region. Neither the USSR nor China wanted a war over Korea, and both were happy to reach an agreement that ended the conflict.

COUNTING THE COST

The Cold War was played out in a deadly land and air war in Korea. Soviet MiG-15 fighter planes, some piloted by Soviet pilots, fought American F-86 Sabers. Terrible atrocities occurred on both sides, and the U.S. Air Force dropped almost as many bombs on the cities of North Korea as had been dropped on Germany over the entire course of World War II. Peace talks began in late 1951 and dragged on until a final ceasefire took effect in July 1953. Millions of Korean civilians and

BELOW *UN soldiers head north to engage in fighting while Korean civilians flee south with their possessions to escape the battlefront.*

soldiers, at least a quarter of a million Chinese, more than 54,000 Americans, and 3,000 other UN troops all lost their lives in the war.

WAR IN VIETNAM

Beginning shortly after the Korean War, the U.S. became involved in another part of Asia for much the same reason that had led to its presence in Korea. The country this time was Vietnam, a former French colony that was divided into two halves in 1954 after France suffered a military defeat by Vietnamese rebels fighting for independence. The northern half of the country came under a communist government, while the southern half of the country was left in the hands of non-communist Vietnamese groups who had backed France. South Vietnam, an undemocratic state where elections never took place, was backed by the U.S., which wanted to contain the spread of communism in southeast Asia.

A guerrilla war developed as Vietnamese rebels sought to unite the country's south with the north. In 1965, the U.S. sent marines to South Vietnam, and by the end of the year, with more than 200,000 American troops in the country, the Vietnam War had begun. Nationalist forces supporting North Vietnam in both halves of the country became known as the Viet Cong.

RIGHT *This poster, printed in North Vietnam in the middle of the Vietnam War, appealed to nationalist feelings with the words, "Strive to train soldiers to defend the nation."*

RA SỨC RÈN LUYỆN QUÂN SỰ SẴN SÀNG BẢO VỆ TỔ QUỐC

? EVENT IN QUESTION

The Domino Theory: A myth?

The fall of one domino can have an effect on a whole row of dominoes. This example was used to argue that the loss of one state to Soviet communism would lead to eventual domination by the USSR of a whole series of countries. This domino theory became the logic for conducting the war in Vietnam and for the Cold War as a whole, but the logic has been questioned by many historians. The Viet Cong were not Soviet puppets but nationalists who fought to remove foreign powers from their land. It has also been pointed out that although the Viet Cong were victorious, this did not have the destabilizing effect in southeast Asia that many predicted. One domino fell, but it did not lead to a collapse of the whole row of dominoes. Some people claim the domino theory was an excuse for the U.S. to try to dominate the world.

THE CONFLICT CONTINUES

American involvement in Vietnam gradually increased in its scope, and by 1967 there were more than 400,000 American troops in South Vietnam. Meanwhile, the Viet Cong received assistance from China and the Soviet Union.

The launch of a major offensive by the Viet Cong in 1968, the Tet offensive, proved to be a failure, but the large scale and unexpected nature of the attack convinced many U.S. leaders that the war was unwinnable. It took another five years before this was generally accepted in the U.S., and a peace settlement was finally reached in 1973. Two years later, South Vietnam was invaded and overrun by the North Vietnamese, and the country was unified as a single communist nation.

A COSTLY FAILURE

American involvement in Vietnam was largely viewed as a failure, both internationally and within the U.S. It raised moral questions about American policy towards small, developing countries that bore the brunt of Cold War hostilities. Moral questions were also raised when it became known that U.S. leaders had agreed to heavy bombing of Cambodia and Laos (neighbors of Vietnam that the North Vietnamese used for their supply lines) without the knowledge of the American public. The deaths of thousands of American soldiers came to be seen by many as pointless and unnecessary. In the U.S. itself, many young people rebelled when drafted to fight in a war in which they did not believe.

PEOPLE IN QUESTION

Ho Chi Minh
(1892–1969)

Ho Chi Minh was the leader of the Viet Cong who fought the Americans in Vietnam. During the 1960s, he was viewed by many in the West as a dangerous enemy, dedicated to spreading communism across south-east Asia. Today, many historians regard Ho Chi Minh as first and foremost a nationalist who wanted Vietnam to be an independent country. He was a communist, but not one who worked for the USSR in the Cold War. He did seek help from both the USSR and China, but only because he needed their support in his country's struggle for independence.

ABOVE *A Vietnamese mother and her children swim across a river at Quinhon in South Vietnam to escape a U.S. air strike at the start of the Vietnam War in 1965.*

35

WAR IN AFGHANISTAN

The events in Afghanistan are an example of how the post-Vietnam Cold War was conducted by the U.S. and the USSR. In 1979, Afghanistan was ruled by a communist government that did not have the support of Afghans and was propped up by the USSR. The U.S. gave secret support to Afghan opposition, and in order to crush this opposition, the USSR sent in troops to occupy the country.

A bitter civil war developed, with the CIA providing many millions of dollars to the Mujahedeen, the name of the Islamic fighters who resisted the Soviet occupation. The national security adviser to the U.S. president at that

BELOW *Soviet troops in Afghanistan two days after the first and only violation of a neutral border by the USSR during the Cold War.*

time, Jimmy Carter, later spoke of giving the USSR its own Vietnam, and the Soviet experience in Afghanistan did have similarities to American involvement in Vietnam. In both conflicts, the invading forces gradually became more and more committed to a guerrilla war that they couldn't win.

By the end of 1982, nearly 5,000 Soviet soldiers had died in Afghanistan, and the USSR was ready to withdraw. The war did not end, however, until the Cold War itself drew to a close. The Mujahedeen continued fighting, this time amongst themselves, until a group known as the Taliban emerged to rule most of the country and form their own government.

ABOVE *The Mujahedeen, or "soldiers of God," rebelled against a left-wing government in Afghanistan that encouraged women to join literacy classes. They recruited boys and armed them with AK-47 rifles.*

❓ EVENT IN QUESTION

The rise of the Taliban: A result of the Cold War?

From one point of view, the Taliban was a group of ruthless and extremist Afghan fighters. As rulers of Afghanistan, they were heavily financed by Osama bin Laden, a wealthy Saudi Arabian who became fiercely anti-American. Some historians argue that the Taliban was a monster hatched by the Cold War. If the USSR and the U.S. had not turned Afghanistan into a theater of war, it is unlikely that an extremist group like the Taliban would ever have emerged. Those Mujahedeen who became the Taliban were united by Islam and a common desire to expel Soviet troops. One reason they grew strong was because of the funding they received from the U.S. over the course of the Cold War.

CHAPTER 4

Living through the Cold War

The Cuban missile crisis (see pages 18–19) had a sobering effect on both superpowers. If nuclear weapons were used by either side, the only certain result would be the death of millions. This led to a theory that nuclear peace could be maintained because of, and not merely in spite of, the certainty of mutually assured destruction (MAD). For many people living through the Cold War, the MAD theory came to seem an appropriate name for an insane state of affairs in which the destruction of the planet was the only certain outcome of World War III.

A BREAK IN HOSTILITIES

Some periods of the Cold War promised the possibility of peaceful co-existence between the superpowers. One such period came after the superpowers accepted a divided Europe, a divided Germany, and a divided city of Berlin. In 1958, at the start of what would be a three-year period free of nuclear testing, negotiations for a test ban treaty got underway but failed because the two sides could not agree over how best to proceed. Meetings between the USSR and the U.S. took place in the early 1970s and led to the signing of two treaties in 1972. They were known as SALT-I (Strategic Arms Limitation Talks) and limited the quantity of nuclear weapons each side could stockpile. Further agreements led to a SALT-II treaty in 1979, but by this time

? WHAT IF...

There was a Dr. Strangelove?

In 1964, Hollywood released a film called *Dr. Strangelove, or How I Learned to Stop Worrying and Love the Bomb.* In the film, the commander of a U.S. air base goes insane and orders a nuclear attack on the USSR. The attack is called off, but, due to a series of mishaps, one bomber plane cannot be recalled. The Soviets are warned, but they are unable to prevent their own defense system, a "Doomsday machine," from automatically releasing nuclear weapons as a response to being attacked. The film ends with a series of nuclear explosions, and the audience imagines the end of the world. Critics of the film insisted that, in the real world, safety features would ensure that such a catastrophic situation could never take place. Others argued that a Doomsday machine was technically possible and that the likelihood of a terrible mistake being made was always a real possibility.

the Cold War was heating up again, and the treaty was never ratified by the U.S. Senate.

In the U.S., a more aggressive attitude toward the USSR became associated with Ronald Reagan's election as president in 1980. The USSR was also shifting to a more hostile attitude. Both sides began developing new nuclear weapons systems: the SS-20 missiles by the Soviets, and Pershing-2 and Cruise missiles by the Americans. In the early 1980s, the Reagan administration engaged the USSR in an intensive arms race and announced plans to develop a new defense system against incoming missiles, popularly known as "Star Wars."

ABOVE *U.S. President Richard Nixon and Russian Communist Party leader Leonid Brezhnev shake hands after signing the SALT-I treaty in 1972.*

PROPAGANDA WAR

Throughout the Cold War, a propaganda war developed between the two superpowers. This involved each side seeking to portray itself as morally superior to the other. The U.S. presented itself as standing for freedom in the face of a Soviet communist dictatorship that denied human rights. The USSR presented itself as standing for a just society in the face of a capitalist America that placed profit above equality.

Words and images, including books and films, became the weapons of the propaganda war. In the USSR, books and films were promoted that focused on social injustices in the West such as racial inequality and poverty. Books by a Russian author, Aleksandr Solzhenitsyn, that featured Soviet prison camps and the abuse of state power were translated into English and widely promoted in the West. Some of the most widely read novels in the West were Cold War thrillers featuring spies and traitors, which usually portrayed the "bad guys" as working for the USSR and the "good guys" as working for the West.

BELOW This 1957 advertisement for American Convair F-102A jet planes, like the Soviet cartoon on page 5, is an example of the propaganda war that was an essential part of the Cold War.

Freedom Has a New Sound!

ALL OVER AMERICA these days the blast of supersonic flight is shattering the old familiar sounds of city and countryside.

At U.S. Air Force bases strategically located near key cities our Airmen maintain their *round the clock* vigil, ready to take off on a moment's notice in jet aircraft like Convair's F-102A all-weather interceptor. Every flight has only one purpose—your personal protection!

The next time jets thunder overhead, remember that the pilots who fly them are not wilful disturbers of your peace; they are patriotic young Americans affirming your *New Sound of Freedom!*

PUBLISHED FOR BETTER UNDERSTANDING OF THE MISSION OF THE U.S.A.F. AIR DEFENSE COMMAND

CONVAIR

THE ENEMY WITHIN

In real life, some traitors were paid for betraying their government's secrets, while others sincerely believed that they were working for a country that represented a better way of life. Early on in the Cold War, there were Soviet spies with high-ranking positions in the British secret service. Men such as Guy Burgess and Kim Philby passed on valuable secrets to the KGB, the Soviet equivalent of the CIA. Later in the Cold War, Oleg Gordievsky, working for the KGB in London, passed valuable information to the West. People lost their lives as a result of spying. Philby identified agents working for the West, who were caught and shot. In

America, Ethel and Julius Rosenberg were executed in the electric chair after being found guilty of passing atomic secrets to the USSR.

? EVENT IN QUESTION

Flight 007: Who was at fault?

In August 1983, a Korean Airlines passenger plane, Flight 007, was shot down with the loss of 269 lives. A Soviet fighter plane brought down the jumbo jet, which was 367 miles (587 km) off course and inside a sensitive area of Soviet air space. The incident was highly controversial because while the U.S. condemned it as a terrorist attack, the USSR accused the U.S. of using the passenger plane as part of a spying mission. There was a U.S. surveillance plane in the area at the time, and tapes later revealed that the jumbo jet repeatedly ignored warnings from the Soviet fighter plane, even after shots were fired across it. What was the real cause of the shooting down of Flight 007? The truth may never be known.

BELOW *The family of a Flight 007 victim, shown in her college graduation photograph, grieves at an altar memorial at the Seoul airport in South Korea.*

THE HOUSE UN-AMERICAN ACTIVITIES COMMITTEE

During the Cold War, some American citizens found themselves accused of being sympathetic to the USSR. In the 1950s in the U.S., the House Un-American Activities Committee (HUAC) publicly investigated people working in Hollywood who might be sympathetic to communism. The Federal Bureau of Investigation (FBI), headed by J. Edgar Hoover, also dedicated itself to exposing such people, though in a less public manner. Citizens suspected by HUAC or the FBI of being sympathetic to communism— "reds under the bed," as they were called—were likely to lose their jobs and find themselves prevented from obtaining similar work elsewhere.

Citizens in the USSR and Eastern Europe who were under suspicion of not being loyal enough to the Soviet government were also investigated by government departments. The penalties were far more severe than those in the U.S. Hundreds of thousands of people were sent to labor camps, and before Stalin died in 1953, many citizens whose loyalty was questioned were executed by the state.

CITIZENS PROTEST

In Western Europe, an area very likely to be targeted in the event of total war, people began to protest against nuclear weapons. In 1958 in London, the Campaign for Nuclear Disarmament (CND) was founded, and it called for the removal of nuclear weapons from Britain. Similar campaigns were organized in other parts of Europe, and by the late 1970s, when American missiles were being based in Western Europe, anti-nuclear movements were growing in strength. In the U.S., the focus of citizen protest was against the Vietnam War, a war that many Americans came to regard not only as unwinnable but also as unjustifiable. In October 1967, some 75,000 protestors marched against it in Washington, D.C.

? **EVENT IN QUESTION**

Anti-nuclear demonstrators: Soviet puppets?

The anti-nuclear movements that developed across Western Europe in the late 1970s and early 1980s did not choose sides in the Cold War. They felt that the existence of large numbers of American Cruise missiles in Europe was a threat to the chance of peace. Critics of anti-nuclear movements claimed that such movements only served to weaken the West's ability to win the Cold War. It was said that the Soviet Union was happy to support such movements for just such a reason. Peace protestors argued that the removal of the missiles would encourage the Soviets to do the same. On the other side, critics argued that pacifist protestors were being manipulated by Soviet intelligence.

BELOW *Thousands of people regularly gathered outside the U.S. Air Force base at Greenham Common in Britain to protest the installation of nuclear missiles. A women's peace camp was established there as a focus for anti-nuclear protests.*

CHAPTER 5

The End of the Cold War

In the decade after 1975, when mistrust between the super-powers reached a high level, many people wondered how the Cold War could ever come to a peaceful end, let alone when that might happen. Although both superpowers were spending more money on weapons than ever before, the arms race was proving to be more of a burden to the Soviets than to the Americans.

GORBACHEV BREAKS THE ICE

The American economy was much stronger than the Soviet one, and the U.S. could better afford the high cost of increased military spending. The Soviets only weakened their economy further by trying to keep up with American levels of spending on military equipment. One solution was for the USSR to make drastic cuts in its military spending and channel what was saved into the domestic economy. This is what Mikhail Gorbachev, the new Soviet leader, decided had to be done.

? PEOPLE IN QUESTION

Mikhail Gorbachev
(1931–)

Unlike Stalin, Gorbachev was not a dictator and relied on popular support to push through the radical reforms being made to Soviet society. Like most national leaders, he also needed the support of other leaders and politicians. While he usually had both kinds of support, he also had to contend with conservative communists who grew increasingly alarmed at the way the USSR seemed to be surrendering power to its traditional enemy. In August 1989, the Polish communist leader called Gorbachev to ask for advice about sharing government with non-communists. A few days before the Berlin Wall came down, the East German leader also called Gorbachev to ask for advice. On both occasions, Gorbachev's advice was to give way to popular demand. A different leader of the USSR might have advised the use of the military against the public.

The 1985 election of Mikhail Gorbachev as leader of the Communist Party in the USSR marked an important point in the Cold War. Gorbachev represented a younger generation of Russians and was determined to confront the economic problems facing the USSR. He was a communist who wanted to reform his country so that people could enjoy a higher standard of living. He introduced policies of *perestroika* (economic reform) and *glasnost* (openness) and began negotiations with the U.S. over the reduction of nuclear weapons. Early in 1986, Gorbachev made proposals that astonished the rest of the world, speaking of his wish to eliminate all nuclear weapons. As a first step, he suggested the removal of all medium-range nuclear missiles from Europe, an idea that some in the West thought must be some kind of a trick.

BELOW *The traditional parade of Soviet armed power in Red Square took place as usual in 1985, but Gorbachev was ready to act on his declaration, "We want to stop and not continue the arms race."*

ABOVE *After a morning meeting with President Reagan in Geneva in November 1985, Gorbachev called him a "political dinosaur." But during the afternoon, in front of a log fire, they began to get along; it was the beginning of the end of the Cold War.*

LIFTING THE IRON CURTAIN

Before December 1987, when Gorbachev and Reagan met in Washington, the Soviet leader made it clear that he intended to withdraw troops from Afghanistan (see page 36). Partly as a result, a treaty was signed in Washington that removed all Soviet SS-20 missiles and all American Cruise and Pershing missiles from Europe.

At the end of 1988, Gorbachev astonished the world again by declaring to the UN that the Soviet army would be reduced by half a million men, and that 50,000 soldiers would be removed from Eastern Europe. The consequences of this were profound because the Cold War had always been conducted by each side using military power, or the threat of such power, to maintain control over particular regions. Eastern Europe had been under Soviet control since the end of World War II, but Gorbachev lifted the "Iron Curtain" when he addressed the UN and said, "Force or the threat of force neither can nor should be instruments of foreign policy. . . . Freedom of choice is a universal principle. It knows no exception." Stressing that this applied "both to the capitalist and socialist system," Gorbachev was in effect announcing the USSR's withdrawal from the Cold War.

? WHAT IF...

Gorbachev had not come to power?

What if there was no Gorbachev to meet President George Bush in 1989 and declare, "We don't consider you as an enemy any more"? In one sense it was clearly Gorbachev who brought the Cold War to an end because he took the initiative in ending the arms race and reducing the Soviet military presence in Eastern Europe. In another sense, it could be said that the Cold War was brought to an end by the failure of the Soviet economic system. Gorbachev, desperate to save his country's economy, was forced to end the Cold War because this was the only way to reduce the cost of the military budget. Would the Cold War have ended if Gorbachev had not been the leader of the USSR? What does seem likely is that, without Gorbachev, there would have been far less chance of the Cold War ending as peacefully as it did.

BELOW *Gorbachev and Reagan in Red Square, Moscow, 1988.*

INDEPENDENCE FOR EASTERN EUROPE

The Cold War began to draw to a close in 1989 as countries in Eastern Europe realized the Soviet Union would not use force to maintain its control over them. By the summer of 1989, a non-communist party was sharing power in Poland. By the middle of the year, three Baltic states inside the USSR—Lithuania, Latvia, and Estonia—were demanding independence. The spirit of reform and change that Gorbachev had introduced was having unexpected consequences, as non-Russian states within the USSR called for independence.

THE WALL COMES DOWN

The most dramatic consequence of Gorbachev's reforms was a series of events that led to the knocking down of the Berlin Wall, the most obvious symbol of the Cold War. It started with Hungary's decision to open its border with

BELOW *Drawing back the Iron Curtain, part one: in May 1989, Hungarian border guards cut and pull down the barbed wire fence dividing their country from Austria, allowing East Germans to travel through Czechoslovakia and into Austria via Hungary.*

LEFT *Drawing back the Iron Curtain, part two: in November 1989, the Berlin Wall is brought down for good. The Reichstag, the old German parliament, is in the background.*

non-communist Austria, allowing East Germans to make their way to Hungary and then cross to the West. Some 13,000 people left within three days of the border opening in September 1989. What was happening in Hungary had a major effect on people in East Berlin who also wanted to travel to the West. Large crowds gathered in Berlin on the night of November 9 after an announcement earlier in the day that visas would be granted to all citizens wishing to visit the West. On hearing this promise, people began to demand to cross immediately, and some guards, not sure what to do, opened the gates in the Berlin Wall. Families that had been divided since the Wall went up in 1961 were reunited, and Berlin erupted into emotional celebrations as people began to physically dismantle the Wall.

❓ WHAT IF...

The Cold War never happened?

By the 1980s, some four decades into the Cold War, Soviet citizens often had to line up for essential food items, and many consumer goods were in short supply. In the U.S., where life expectancy for a black person in New York's Harlem was lower than that in some developing countries, the difference between the rich and poor was four times greater than in the USSR. If there had been no Cold War, would some of the trillions of dollars that went into military spending have been spent on problems such as these? It is difficult to know, but what is certain is that many of the millions of people who died in conflicts fueled by superpower rivalry would still be alive today if the Cold War had never taken place. Military spending became a national priority for the superpowers at the expense of social and economic problems, and many other countries affected by the Cold War adopted similar priorities.

THE COLD WAR IS OVER

By the end of 1989, nearly every state in Eastern Europe allied to the USSR had removed its communist rulers. It was remarkable that after so many wars marked the course of the Cold War, its ending was brought about so peacefully. Apart from violent events in Romania that led to the execution of the state's leader, Nicolae Ceausescu, the changes were largely achieved without bloodshed. After the fall of the Berlin Wall, dramatic events continued to unfold as the consequences of Gorbachev's reforms had more unexpected results.

By the middle of 1990, plans for the reunification of Germany had been drawn up, and Gorbachev accepted that Germany would become part of NATO. To many observers, this represented not just the end of the Cold War, but the victory of the West. NATO had been formed as a military alliance against the USSR, and now a united

BELOW *April 1991 and the journey home for Soviet missile launchers that had been based in Poland during the Cold War.*

Germany was going to join that alliance. At the height of the Cuban crisis, Khruschev had written an emotional letter to Kennedy in which he compared the Cold War to two men holding a rope with a knot tied in the middle: "the more the two of us pull, the tighter the knot will be tied." This is how the Cold War seemed to be until Gorbachev arrived on the scene and cut the knot.

BELOW *A portrait of Lenin, the first leader of the USSR, is deliberately spattered with red paint as a gesture of contempt by demonstrators outside the Communist Party building in Kiev, the capital of Ukraine, in August 1991. The Ukrainian demonstrators reaffirmed their country's declaration of independence from the USSR, first made in 1990.*

? EVENT IN QUESTION

The Cold War: Who were the winners?

In many ways, the Cold War was won by the United States. Its economy was more able to support the increasing cost of an arms race, and this was finally acknowledged by the USSR. The West also won the Cold War in the sense that the people of Eastern Europe chose not to support the Soviet Union and chose instead an economic and social system modeled on that of the U.S. A different perspective points out that to speak of winning or losing is itself part of the confrontational vocabulary of the Cold War. Is talk of winning or losing a mature response when the Cold War threatened to destroy all of civilization? Did the USSR achieve a moral victory by choosing to question what was more important—superpower status in a nuclear world or a more modest existence without the need for nuclear weapons?

CHAPTER 6

After the Cold War

I t is not possible to pin down the start of the Cold War to one particular year. The end of World War II in 1945 marks its beginning, although some historians look to 1917 and the Russian communist revolution. This revolution, it is said, marked the start of a deep conflict between two economic and social systems, a conflict that led to the Cold War when both the U.S. and the USSR became superpowers after 1945. The Cold War drew to a close between 1989 and 1991, as the events of those years dramatically changed the course of world history and ended more than 45 years of open hostility between the superpowers.

BELOW *Russia, adopting the Western economic system after the break-up of the USSR, experienced food lines as wages failed to increase in line with price rises.*

LEFT *Capitalism in Russia brought a new range of consumer goods to those who could afford to pay the high prices.*

THE END OF THE USSR

Gorbachev had set out with the intention of ending the Cold War, but he was as surprised as the rest of the world at some of the consequences of his actions and decisions. He believed that the communist states of the USSR and those in Eastern Europe could survive the end of the Cold War as a united body. Money spent on weapons, he thought, would be used instead to strengthen the Soviet economy and deliver a better standard of living for its citizens. Strict government controls would be relaxed, people would be happier, and a socialist USSR would coexist peacefully with a capitalist America. What Gorbachev had not anticipated was that his reforms would lead to the breakup of the Soviet empire and the removal of its communist governments.

? EVENT IN QUESTION

Did the USSR fall, or was it pushed?

The Cold War did not come to an end because one side achieved a decisive military victory. The U.S. did, however, win an important economic victory in that it was more able than the USSR to support the huge cost of conducting the Cold War. From one viewpoint, this proved that an economy like that of the U.S., based on private ownership and profit, was better than an economy like the Soviet one that was based around state ownership. At the same time, it may have been true that the U.S. deliberately set out to break the Soviet economy. Did the U.S. increase the pace of the arms race so that the Soviet economy would be forced to try to keep up with it? This is hard to determine one way or the other. In the early 1980s, however, the U.S. did set out to weaken the Soviet economy by denying it trade with the West and holding back Western financial credit and new computer technology.

Boris Yeltsin, with papers in his hand, prepares to call upon Russians to reject the attempted seizure of power by Soviet conservatives in August 1991. Yeltsin eventually emerged as the new leader of post-Cold War Russia.

"A COMMON VICTORY"

The last thing Gorbachev expected was for the USSR itself to break up and abandon communism, yet this was what unfolded in 1991. Gorbachev and his supporters hoped that, once the Cold War was over, the West would be willing to aid the USSR in the form of large loans. This did not happen, making it more difficult for Gorbachev to deal with critics who felt that the USSR had made too many concessions to the West. On August 19, 1991, a group of Soviet conservatives seized power in Moscow, and Gorbachev, who was away on vacation, was placed under house arrest. The conservatives failed in their attempt, however, and Gorbachev was released. When he returned to Moscow, he found that a new leader, Boris Yeltsin, had emerged.

Yeltsin now campaigned for the breakup of the USSR and a non-communist government for an independent Russia. By the end of 1991, the USSR had ceased to exist as its various states, including Russia, became independent countries.

The Cold War ended as it had begun: with a redrawing of Europe's map. Gorbachev, no longer a world leader, said at the beginning of 1992, "I do not regard the end of the Cold War as a victory for one side. . . . The end of the Cold War is our common victory." That may be true, but for Gorbachev, who did so much to end the conflict, there was to be no place in a post-Cold War Europe.

? EVENT IN QUESTION

After the Cold War: Is the world a safer place?

The fact that the Cold War is over, a part of history, might suggest that the world is now a safer place. Superpowers no longer threaten one another with missiles, nor do they fuel wars in various parts of the world in an attempt to weaken one another.

At the same time, however, as Russia's leader Vladimir Putin said toward the end of 2001, "The Cold War is over. The world has become much more complicated." New international conflicts have risen from the ashes of Cold War conflicts and, it could be argued, are more difficult to resolve because they cannot be controlled in the way they once were by the superpowers.

In the past, regional conflicts around the world were affected by the larger conflict between the U.S. and the USSR. The balance of power between the superpowers meant that neither side wanted a regional conflict to get out of control, and they acted to police such conflicts in ways that would benefit their own interests. Is the world safer without such a balance of power?

ABOVE *At the Cu Chi Revolutionary Martyrs Cemetery outside Ho Chi Minh City, Tran Thi Buon mourns at the grave of her husband, one of the victims of the Cold War, who died 34 years earlier while fighting U.S. and South Vietnamese forces.*

COUNTING THE COST

It is hard to quantify the financial cost of the Cold War, but the superpowers stored many thousands of nuclear bombs and maintained huge armies of men and equipment. The U.S., for example, was spending an average of $400 billion on its defense budget each year, and one estimate for the total cost to both sides of their weapons during the Cold War is $8 trillion ($8,000,000,000,000).

Another cost of the Cold War is measured in the number of human lives that it claimed. Millions of Koreans and Vietnamese died. More than a million Afghans lost their lives, along with thousands of Soviet soldiers fighting in Afghanistan. Hundreds of thousands died in Angola, and many tens of thousands in Central and South America. Thousands of people also died in Romania and Hungary. Russian tanks killed protestors in Czechoslovakia in 1968, and nearly 200 people died trying to cross into West Berlin. Around a quarter of a million Chinese died in Korea, as well as more than 3,000 people of mainly British, Australian, and Turkish nationality making up the UN force. More than 100,000 Americans died fighting foreign wars, and four American students died at Kent State University protesting against the Vietnam War.

EVENT IN QUESTION

The avoidance of nuclear war: Good judgment or good fortune?

What didn't happen in the Cold War—a nuclear war—is, in one sense, more important than what did happen. From the ruins of a devastated Europe and an unstable Asia in 1945, two armed superpowers confronted one another. Each side was suspicious of the intentions of the other, and they jostled uneasily for power in an uncertain world. The U.S. and the USSR learned to respect each other's nuclear capabilities and became better at avoiding direct confrontation. Each side learned to exercise caution, and an uneasy world peace was maintained for more than 40 years. At the same time, though, many wars were fought, and millions died all around the world. The fact that nuclear weapons were never used, it could be argued, was as much luck as anything else. There was always the possibility of an accident, a misunderstanding, or a deliberate choice leading to someone pressing a button, releasing a nuclear missile and setting off a retaliatory attack.

ABOVE *A serviceman keeps watch over military aircraft, once weapons of the USSR, that were destroyed as part of a post-Cold War agreement on the reduction of arms.*

THE LEGACY

BELOW *The world is not necessarily a safer place today. U.S. Navy aircraft during training off the coast of Taiwan in 1996, as China began new live-fire war games in the Taiwan Strait.*

Part of the cost of living through the Cold War was the general fear it created around the world that, at any time, a conflict situation involving the superpowers could develop into a crisis resulting in the use of nuclear weapons. The international, anti-nuclear peace movements that developed in the 1980s were a response to the climate of fear and uncertainty created in a world at the mercy of Cold War politics. The ending of the Cold War, a largely peaceful event, lifted this cloud of fear and

made the world seem a safer place. This is perhaps the greatest legacy of the Cold War.

But not every part of the world has shaken off its legacy from the Cold War. Korea remains a divided country, and Cuba is still regarded with hostility by the U.S. When China became independent in 1949, a small non-communist force fled to the Chinese island of Taiwan and received support from America. The U.S. came to recognize Taiwan's claim to be an independent state, much to China's annoyance, and this remains an unresolved issue. The end of the Cold War has not brought peace to the world. The problems of the Middle East, and the fighting between the Palestinians and Israelis, have not been made any easier to resolve even though the Cold War is over. The Cold War is over, but nuclear weapons still exist and could still be used. Indeed, there is now less control over the use of nuclear weapons than there was during the Cold War.

? EVENT IN QUESTION

A fight for freedom or a fight for power?

For some, the Cold War was a struggle between America's stand for freedom and what President Reagan called an "evil empire." It was a battle of ideas that saw the triumph of freedom when citizens pulled down the Berlin Wall. Other historians, pointing to the way in which democracies were overthrown and countries invaded by the U.S., regard this interpretation as very one-sided.

Some historians say that the two superpowers were much alike, agreeing to control different regions of the world and fighting wars whenever agreement could not be reached. Others argue that the USSR only wanted to defend itself and that it was the U.S. who wanted to expand its power and influence. Was the Cold War a struggle between different belief systems, or was it a struggle for power that ended when one economy proved stronger? There can be no one explanation that simply sums up the Cold War.

Timeline

1945
APRIL 25: American and Soviet soldiers meet on the Elbe River in Germany.

1945
MAY 7: Germany surrenders, and World War II comes to an end in Europe.

1945
AUGUST 6 and 9: Atomic bombs dropped on two Japanese cities.

1945
SEPTEMBER 2: Japan surrenders, and World War II comes to an end in Asia.

1948
JUNE 18: A new western Germany currency is introduced.

1948
JUNE 22: A new eastern Germany currency is introduced.

1948
JUNE 24: The blockade of Berlin begins, and two days later, the first airlift arrives in western Berlin.

1949
MAY 12: The blockade of Berlin is lifted by the Soviet Union.

1949
OCTOBER 1: China becomes an independent country.

1950
JUNE 25 : South Korea is invaded by North Korea.

1953
JULY 27: A ceasefire signals the end of the Korean War.

1954
JUNE: The government of Guatemala is overthrown by a CIA-trained guerrilla force, and a military government is established.

1956
NOVEMBER: A Hungarian uprising is crushed by Soviet forces.

1959
JANUARY 8: Castro forms a new government in Cuba after the overthrow of a dictatorship.

1961
AUGUST 13: East Germany decides to begin building a barrier between East and West Berlin. This becomes the Berlin Wall.

1961
APRIL 13: A failed invasion of Cuba, planned by the CIA, gets underway.

1962
OCTOBER 14: A U.S. spy plane photographs missile sites under construction in Cuba.

1962
OCTOBER 27: Kennedy and Khruschev come to a peaceful agreement over Cuba, and the Soviet missiles are withdrawn.

1965
FEBRUARY: Heavy U.S. bombing of North Vietnam begins.

1965
APRIL: U.S. invasion of the Dominican Republic.

1967
JUNE: The Six-Day War between Israel and the Arab states of Egypt, Jordan, and Syria.

1968
MARCH: U.S. announces its decision to withdraw from Vietnam and seek peace.
AUGUST: Soviet forces intervene in Czechoslovakia.

1969
NOVEMBER: Strategic Arms Limitation Talks (SALT) begin in Helsinki.

1972
FEBRUARY: President Nixon meets Mao Zedong in China.

1973
SEPTEMBER: President Allende of Chile is overthrown in a coup.

1973
SEPTEMBER 11: President Allende of Chile is killed, and General Pinochet becomes head of a military government.

1973
OCTOBER: The October War, or Yom Kippur War, between Israel, Egypt, and Syria.

1975
APRIL: North Vietnam takes over South Vietnam, and the country is unified.

1975
NOVEMBER: Civil war in Angola, and an invasion by South African troops is defeated by Cuban forces.

1979
JUNE: After a civil war, a Sandinista government is formed in Nicaragua.

1979
DECEMBER: The Soviet invasion of Afghanistan begins.

1981
NOVEMBER: The CIA begins training and arming the Contras to fight the Sandinista government in Nicaragua.

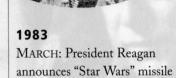

1983
MARCH: President Reagan announces "Star Wars" missile defense system.

1983
OCTOBER: U.S. military intervention in Grenada.

1989
FEBRUARY: Soviet troops withdraw from Afghanistan.

1989
AUGUST: A non-communist government is formed in Poland.

1989
NOVEMBER 9: The Berlin Wall comes down.

1990
OCTOBER: East and West Germany are reunited.

1991
AUGUST: Failed attempt to overthrow Gorbachev in Moscow.

1991
DECEMBER: The USSR ceases to exist.

Glossary

Allies The countries opposing Germany, Japan, and their supporters in World War II.

armory A collection of weapons.

arms race A competitive race to develop a bigger supply of better weapons.

capitalist Supporting the economic system of capitalism, based upon private ownership and the pursuit of profits.

CIA The Central Intelligence Agency of the U.S., a government organization.

colonial Relating to a colony, a country ruled and inhabited by people of a foreign government.

communism The political and economic system of the USSR and Eastern Europe during the Cold War, based upon one-party rule and state control of the economy.

Congress The part of the U.S. government that passes new laws.

conservatives In politics, people who don't want to make changes.

dictatorship A state under the control of a ruler with unlimited authority.

diplomatic relations Peaceful channels of communication between countries through embassies.

Eastern Europe During the Cold War, this referred to European countries that had communist governments and were supported by the USSR.

guerrilla war A war between an independent, and usually political, force and larger regular forces, often representing a government.

Iron Curtain A term that came to describe the closed border between Eastern and Western Europe during the Cold War.

KGB The USSR's intelligence organization, established to help conduct the Cold War.

labor camp A prison camp based around hard labor.

left-wing In politics, relating to people who want to make changes.

liberal reforms The relaxation of laws, usually economic and social laws, that are regarded as too strict.

medium-range nuclear missiles Nuclear weapons capable of traveling a medium range (within a continent rather than between continents).

Mujahedeen Islamic fighters who resisted the Soviet occupation of Afghanistan between 1979 and 1989.

national security advisor A person appointed to inform and advise the U.S. president on matters of national security.

nationalist patriot A person with principles supporting a policy of national independence.

nationalize To take over the private ownership of an industry or business on behalf of a nation and its government.

NATO North Atlantic Treaty Organization, formed by the West to conduct the Cold War.

Nazism The political and racist system of Hitler's Germany between 1933 and 1945.

pacifist Someone who believes that war and violence are not a solution to disputes and that they can be settled by peaceful means.

patriotism Strong and devoted support of one's country.

propaganda Information or misinformation designed to promote a point of view.

retaliatory Responding to an attack by launching a counterattack of a similar kind.

revolution Far-reaching change, often involving the overthrow of a government or a social order.

Russia *see* USSR.

SALT Strategic Arms Limitation Talks, starting with SALT-1 in the early 1970s.

socialism A left-wing, non-communist set of political and social ideas.

superpower A state with supreme power and influence, such as the U.S. and the USSR during the Cold War.

Further Information

supply lines Routes used for providing supplies and weapons during a war.

Taliban The Islamic group that emerged to form a government after Afghanistan's civil war following the withdrawal of Soviet troops.

United Nations An international peace-seeking organization made up of representatives of most of the world's nations.

USSR The Union of Socialist Soviet Republics, the communist state set up in 1917 and disbanded in 1991.

Warsaw Pact Formed by the USSR and Eastern Europe to conduct the Cold War (equivalent of NATO in the West).

West In international politics, countries such as the U.S., many European states, and Japan. The Cold War pitted the West against the East (the USSR and Eastern Europe).

BOOKS

Hatt, Christine. *The End of the Cold War*. London: Hodder Wayland, 2002.

Isaacs, Jeremy, and Taylor Downing. *The Cold War*. London: Transworld Publishing, 1998.

Isaacs, Jeremy, et al. *Cold War: An Illustrated History, 1945–1991*. New York: Little Brown & Co., 1998.

Lafeber, Walter. *America, Russia, and the Cold War, 1945–2002*. New York: McGraw Hill, 2002.

McCauley, Martin. *Russia, America and the Cold War, 1949–1991*. New York: Longman, 1998.

Nathan, James A., ed. *The Cuban Missile Crisis Revisited*. New York: Palgrave Macmillan, 1993.

Ross, Stewart. *The Cold War: Causes*. London: Hodder Wayland, 2001.

Taylor, David. *20th Century Perspectives: The Cold War*. Oxford: Heinemann Library, 2001.

Walker, Martin. *The Cold War*. New York: Henry Holt & Co., 1993.

Index